in the
Mother Tongue

in the
Mother-Tongue

Catherine Anderson

Alice James Books   Cambridge, Massachusetts

The publication of this book was made possible with support from the Massachusetts Council on the Arts and Humanities, a state agency whose funds are recommended by the Governor and appropriated by the State Legislature.

Library of Congress Catalogue Card Number 83-08-2377
ISBN 0-914086-46-4 (paperback)
ISBN 0-914086-47-2 (hardbound)
Cover design by Carlota Duarte
Book design by Susan Graham
Typesetting by Kathy Mendelson

Alice James Books are published by
the Alice James Poetry Cooperative, Inc.

Alice James Books
138 Mount Auburn Street
Cambridge, Massachusetts   02138

Acknowledgments

I would like to thank the Artists Foundation Inc. for supporting this work during the year 1980-81 and the following publications in which these poems first appeared:

The Antioch Review, *"Amelia"*; Intro #8, ed. by George Garrett. Copyright ©1977 by Anchor Books, *"Raccoon"*; Syracuse Guide: *"Picnic"* under the title *"Luke 37:13"*; Syracuse Poems: *"Grace,"* *"My Grandmother Dreams of Dying Young"*; Tendril: *"This Woman,"* *"Never Leaving the City"*

Thanks also to Kinereth Gensler for her editorial advice in completion of this collection.

For my brother Charlie,
still learning to speak

Contents

I

II

I

One Strand

Still when someone speaks
the word death
you shudder like a child.

Well, what if you had nothing
and wanted to make the kind of music
you heard from a juke box one night
so slow and wild it rolled you over
and made you yell out honey to the sky?
You'd take a wire from a broom,
wouldn't you, nail it to the front wall
of your mother's house,
slide a rock down it for tone,
use the neck of a bottle
and a sliver of birch.

And once you'd made it,
you'd stand there as hollow
as the wind which carries gasoline
and pine on it.
You'd pause a long time there,
in her house,
not touching the one strand you've
placed exactly so these pineboard walls
could buzz like a guitar,
the notes rising high and unsullied
over gravel and chickweed;
you'd be like a midwife
touching nothing except the wind
drying her hands slowly
the long hour before birth.

The River Is Part of the Sky

I

A musician who played
like Louis Armstrong
pushed the sunglasses back
on his bald head
and it became jazz season
in a city park named after an island.
Chinese lanterns swayed over
the river dock, over the crowd
and soloists.
In the distance, one beam
swept water and then the sky,
lighting a corridor for jets
in their luminous ascent
away from us.

II

When Detroit City burned its
terrible wick to ash,
I wanted to remember
how a dog shook water off its back
like a rainfall.
It was the same water entering a river,
up the sky, through the clouds,
and down again,
in rain.
And when the rain went
somewhere else, the river
became part of the sky,
a dark space in a musician's throat,
one long tube of sound, hollowing,
as if there could be no poverty
in air carried by voice,
no silence to a man arranging himself
underneath a cement viaduct in August,
his tenor sax poised, the final
gesture pain shapes a pair of hands
when they hold almost nothing.

Never Leaving the City

You turn back down the road
which intersects somewhere downtown
past shoes and wire,
past swollen elm roots breaking cement
like glass. Out of contempt
these trees would live longer
than the road,
or the sooted bricks, or
the dray horses who resembled them.

Because you remember
an abandoned coffee factory
on the left corner, next to a field
of late summer chicory
blooming over the ankles of the last
softball team in August,
the sky may keep a gray ball
in threshold,
as far as the arm extends,
and a friend may be watching from the third floor,
holding the window open with her shoulders
as she yells your name.
This is memory,
the sky releasing your wonderful return.
All things are the same,
the players breaking up for home,
carrying a ball between their knuckles
through anything like time,
the anger of trees,
or another bad winter of love.

40 Nights on a River Barge

for my brother Bill

Six hours on and six hours off,
and before your last shift of sleep,
the Ohio river could easily turn itself back
until the slow shoulders working alongside you
become the banked hills of Indiana,
two long brown slopes on either side
and a wood freckling downstream.
This is your final haul home,
switchback over the skin of an aging country.
The Union Army once buried their prisoners
sitting upright here in the shallow banks,
one head touching another, bending leeward.
All spring they seem to sweat with you
into the water,
as if the rain settling around your neck
could never be as lasting as their breath.

Jonas

We were threshing envelope after white envelope
on a conveyor in redundant Detroit,
your sons bought you twenty-four Dutch Masters,

Jonas Raimundas,

one hangs from your lip like a bitten sausage.
It is amazing how your mouth moves around it;
you are speaking Lithuanian to the gears,
and to me you are saying again
how they first shot your mother and then your father.
You rolled their muslin wrapped bodies to the sea
because it was January;
you were fifteen,
your shoulders could not break the earth,
and now, at night, you believe
the Baltic is rising over there while
you are here.
Your uncles have always said
you have dark hair,
the color of your mother's,
and eyes, too,
as blue, as deep as ikons.

For Lack of Words: 1957

It is left in the brown overcoat.
You cannot recall your wife's hair,
the rain and whisky dropping off like shoes.
You are forgetting the names of cigarettes,
the names of your children.
This is the morning you wish the dog would talk.
For lack of words, you think of the plants
in the window turning to you,
clasping their brown luggage like worried immigrants.
Look, Hungarians are everywhere,
the house is swelling,
and you are the conductor moving from room to room
passing out licorice.

Wax Wings

Go take your son fishing by Grand Traverse Bay
while the water is green,
and he laughs
at twelve years, youngest and short,
but with huge, optimistic feet.
Take him. He will grow into cat-tails
inhaling the breath of lakes.

You are blunt. The brow quivers. Your hair is cottonweed,
but the fish are singing in the water, which means
they are hungry and will bite
when you are ready.

To think plaid fishermen tucked behind elms
wait for Petoskey sunsets
as patiently as the faithful
anticipating miracles at Fatima or Czestochowa.
They are drinking coffee and changing boots,
waiting for their sons to fall out of the sky
in exquisite wax drops.

His Camera

Like a boy with his first gun, she thought.
No different at all.
Sky, wheel, pipe, crates.
When he caught her in the privy,
she wouldn't speak to him all through dinner.
Kitchen table and closet door,
the ice-house reeling out the window.
A hand, a skirt, a shoe at the side.
He couldn't focus.
Objects he saw easily vanished
into a haze he couldn't reach,
the camera tilting
at the ugliest things:
a bald rise above the waterline,
the crooked trash trees,
or a field of battered tires.
When she saw pictures of her children,
their bodies shocked her.
Hair and teeth, torn clothes and nails,
so many fingers, these small people
etched in paper air.

Running Otter's Oath

One bone was like a bridge,
the collar bone lifting the head
into wilderness,
places where the tongue met breath,
naming: Susquehanna,
Cuyahoga, Tuscarawas.
When Chief Running Otter
posed for his last wrestling portrait
in Cleveland, 1937
he did not raise his champion right fist
into the air
or kiss his mother ringside,
even though shadows in the photograph
indicate a grange hall filled with ovation.
Instead, he let his eyes drop halfway closed
as he leaned back against the ropes,
his chest covered in a deerskin
chewed to a limp drape:
White man, your eyes are mud,
your animals barren and colorless,
your rivers filled
with the blood of thieves.
All I want to do
is stand on the highest building in Cleveland,
above your head,
with two drums of hot oil
balanced on nothing
but a board and my neck.

The Gentle Bourgeoisie

Their sleep fills up hundreds of rooms with breath
every night. They are the occupants of space,
and wide, gracious lines.
In their dreams, windows
are breaking without noise.

On Sunday, a woman wearing a tweed coat
speaks softly from a church podium.
She is asking them for money to relieve
a remote population diminishing
to darkness. Over silence, the words
are difficult to form.
Directly to her side, a cascade of lamb faces
hangs suspended between two rough beams.
The congregation listens to her in sympathy.
They are an architecture of innocence,
an alignment of pine and clothing, clothing
and wine light filtered from a colored window.
The gentle woman tugs a string of pearls
around her neck, as if to stop
the urgency in her voice:

Do not compare her to the news photo of another
woman staring over the corpse of her child,
and say her head is like a white lotus, or her
closing fingers, slender stalks of bamboo
bending in a field.
Do not think they are two moons swelling over
the earth in sorrow;
it was not irony which created them together.

A Photograph of Farmworkers

I

Thirty miles from Delano
that sun can bring cups of sweat
over the face, streams of it rolling
from the hairline.
The old mother wraps and unwraps
her swollen fingers to work the rows.
In a field of ripening lettuce
they are all resting for this image
made of graphite and cut silver,
as light as hen feathers.
How much of nothing hair and clothes tell us.
But the sun is imaginable,
a daily weight a person bears
lowered first on haunches, then
rising a thousand times
from the small of the back.

II

The others are faces in still shots,
blurred half smiles,
shadowed and grave above the eyes.
Angelos Sanchez and his mother, wife,
and three tanned daughters.
Last summer they all traveled over the border
with high, fluish fevers.
For miles the oldest girl had to fan
her sister's skin
in the back of a pickup.
It was night-time, and they held their faces
close to the cooling metal floor,
hearing the cracked road bottom,
and the beat of stones
against the truck axle.

III

Now the sky above them is a blue,
tight line.
They would like to laugh,
but they must be serious.
Some of them are shirtless, a few in straw hats.
The women are wearing loose cotton blouses.
All June they have picked lettuce
and tomorrow they will drive to New Mexico
and then toward Oklahoma,
where the land becomes one flat blade,
and the sun is an animal of hair and teeth.
It grasps the flesh on your back,
then claws out of your hand until darkness,
when it hides to sleep.

The Story

How he drove all the way to Cairo
without stopping,
the night migration of wings
beating inward.

How he placed his hand along the underside
of an engine, and
dreamed he was there
so soon.

The wet Illinois grass
parted in half
when he found her lying
with her blouse opened, her legs
bent like junked pipes.
How he brushed the rust off her hair
and eyes because he knew her

and wanted to carry her
with him to a garage
where he could fall to work
on one more old car.
And how, as his fingers moved through
box after box of tools
there on the floor

she watched him become just another person
rising to wash the grease off his hands
in a sink by the window.

A Body of Heart

for Michelle

Early in the morning he would set up
his nickel and dime carousel
in a field of cracked mud and inner tubes.
Over a patch of flattened grass
he could raise his dull tarpaulin
like the Big Tent. Then he would unload
the blue and yellow ponies, lifting
their wooden flanks carefully, as if
he were touching children.
I never knew his name,
but when he lit a cigarette against the wind,
his fingers shaping an arc over his eyes
and mouth, bearing inward, I knew
memory must be a solid weight pulling
blood through skin, the slow fall
of summer through a lifetime.
Then one morning he told me how on his last day of work
reading meters, a malnourished girl
had gripped his shirt when he found her,
wet skin and bones,
locked for years inside a cellar closet.
Seven years old and her head
touched the top of his knee.
These were hardly his hands at all
pulling her out of her own water.
When he carried her on his shoulder up the stairs,
counting backwards in his mind, or praying
for blindness, the white maples outside
were leaning into the alley as if
someone were waiting to catch them.

The heat and stench of her small body
should have gagged his lungs,
but as he put her down near the cellar door,
it was his heart, he said,
which almost fell through his arms.

This Woman

For days I think I've seen her,
wading a young son in a pond beyond the quarry.
She pulls the shirt off his back,
rolls up the cuffs of his pants.
He throws gentle pearls of water at her, then
over her head she swings him, in the air,
over the water,
as if he were nothing, not
this taut, dark body and its rolling yell,
not those glistening boy muscles,
but some oblique wheel of her soul,
in its turning,
in its sorrow.

I think she carries those beads of pond water
in her hair 13 miles
to a highway club
where she dances in a pale gown
all night, without taking it off.
For the money, she says, for the practice,
because to take it off is
to lose yourself,
to give away the one true song
belting out of your skin.

But the men don't stop watching,
hands and thighs slapping
to a chunky noise on a juke box.
Tonight they are stupid and tuneless.
In a northern mill town, at the end of summer,
she doesn't care what they want,
soon they will stumble into the night.

In the Mother Tongue

Lost for hours in the widest part of the country,
we came to a civic park outside Santa Fe
where they kept a B-29 from World War II
behind chicken wire,
shot up with holes,
spray painted over rust.
Weeds grew from the tail,
the fuselage settled like a shell into gravel.
Because the pilot seat could not be pried back
from its ejection position,
I could imagine the arc of death:
all sand,
metal, and windless light.
Not a lupine or thistle would breathe in the heat.
The park was vacant except for a family
selling chilies and rosaries
from the back of their station wagon.
When one of the women pulled away from the group
and walked toward us
with the limp grace of a survivor,
a rain cloud widened above us;
we wanted to find the mountains.
As she answered in the open vowels of Spanish,
a voice slipped quietly on its side,
like a plane finding its way through lungs,
a voice which collects itself to rain
once every summer over the desert,
falling soon now over the metal and sand,
filling the throat of an absent pilot.

Amelia

(1889-1937?)

The sinking wings,
my navigator's face
sliced against the engine,
small fish rush to us like children.
My plane recedes into the sand and I
hear the moaning of old whales;
I want to offer the navigator milk, but instead
I shake out the smell of motors from his jacket.
Down here I am giving up.

Falling through the water
was like taking off gloves.
Here, you may have them in California,
with my long legs and my soaked khakis.
Take them. Turn them into laundry. —
If you follow a sink line down
to where the Japanese are siphoning water
from my skull, may you find nothing
but the steel gray of our wings dissolving,
and my eyes, propped graciously toward the sky.
You have no idea how beautiful it is.
When starfish rise to the top like night
I am easily fooled and think of air.

From an Ancestor

Nothing is written of our skin,
the leaning into one another.
The window opens like snow falling into
a landscape of arms and legs;
even out here I am human,
my voice straining a wide field.
Like every good woman, I say,
leave me   leave me
I am brushing the blood off another ewe.

II

Birth of My Brother

Even before they told me
I thought of the creation of snow.
They knew you were coming like this,
your face tilted north.
It was January when you fell all over us;
they said the moon
was spinning off another skin.

When I was young
they had names for you:
Brain-damaged, Cretin,
Boy Who Sees Space.
You inherited vacancy,
a featureless plane of ice
grazing the forehead of an ancestor.

Every winter of your life
I wonder how the ground beginning to stiffen
could never be your pain,
that polar resilience the face requires
before snow.

Raccoon

The animal strains
when the stars align,
gaping, artless.

Entering the raccoon's eye,
I take her breath,
I follow in her legs,
I forget the moon and her uneaten clams,
the locust growing in his shell,
becoming old, bending his legs.

The sky is turning;
we are lost to the wood.
Fallen in the clutch of weeds,
the fur parts, our haunches tremble,
the blood comes,
one by one the creatures burst;
low murmurs and the stars
break to pieces over our body.
We lick them, they learn to breathe,
they settle in our skin.

Reindeer

When you were eighteen you lived with a family of Lapps
who would not speak your name for three months,

but you learned to fill your boots with henna grass
awkwardly at first

while the oldest member of the family laughed at you
behind her hands.

The fourth month she showed you how to work a knife
against the body of a reindeer until you could

pull the severed skin apart yourself
almost blind and without feeling

the liquid freezing over your wrists.

On a day they were losing the sun,
she simply sat down and began carving a piece of horn,

instructing you to do the same because
this was her way of speaking to you

of the herd and how to know the difference
among their thickening bodies,

how fully intimate they are,
yet separate,

the fur oranging to one plane in the failing light,
then parting away as each one catches sight of home.

The skill of carving was one of her lessons
that would come to you later

when you understood that no person should live
in the depth of winter

without another body running beside her.

First Lesson

On earth we have the idea of a circle
because the eye is eternal,
and if I were to give you a conch shell
the shape of your ear,
you would know also the motion of sound
floating in the same direction
as a flock of birds
shifting from one pole to the next.

The earth is no heavier
carried on the back of a mule.
We lesser ones call birth
a theory of motion parting the voice from the body,
a wind rising with the gift of tides.

Sea Graves

When the sun finally
reaches the sea,
a woman follows an embrace
along a narrow acre of pilings
toward land.
She is walking behind the others
packing gear.
Their long, easy reels and their voices
are as far as water.
Above her, white gulls are gaining
a change of light.
She shakes salt from her sleeves
and hair as if she would never
look again toward that lost rise
of earth beyond the shore,
where the shelf slips,
and someone may have fallen once,
facedown, arms streamlined
and tucked into skin.
In this era, a thousand primitive fish
surfacing to the top
look like nothing human,
the blunt confusion of their eyes is meaningless
as they are hauled up and sliced.

Only a Street

Before a storm,
black wires and the shoulders of old men
sway back, without wind.
A grocer cranks his awning shut
over a sidewalk,
a beautician closes every window
of her third story parlor.
Above us now
come the clouds, like pale hooves,
as two neighbors exchange
laundry between their kitchens.
And before the last wet sleeve
can cross the alley,
before the final drop of clothespins
down the line,
before the sky's utterly terrible
and natural collapse,
there will be a moment in this dream
equal to memory,
when I am a child again
naming my fears behind a windowshade.
First, there is the fear of no light,
then there is the fear of no voice,
then there is the fear of the earth
suddenly opening to occupy the sky.

Deucalion and Pyrrha

We will be left like them,
the world under us a great bath,
two good people
& a boat perilously seesawing
on the driest peak.
I won't know what to say
when the ocean gods stop
and the clouds open for us.
Do I ask for children?
When that other god answers,
unclothe yourself and bury your mother,
I will fall to my knees and weep
in the stones,
who look like my daughters,
shivering in rain.

Before There Are Children

The thought of progeny
is something we put away,
there in the womb.
Yet it persists,
the voice of an intruder,
embracing our wet layers.

Like a real child, it clings,
rocking in our blood every season,
and sleeping,
then quietly leaving the membranous cradle.

For once, I would like to reach in
and pull it out for a minute,
to hold what it is,
strange and resonant
that keeps moving between our legs,
parted from the spilled streams of a man
and the sloughed cells of a woman.

I am fascinated by its calling
and I am turning my thighs inside out
to reach it,
the voice as hidden
as the body lying beside me,
folded into my back
and the slope of my hip, breathing
with everything else alive.

Snowfall over the Atlantic

In winter we lie down
and resemble each other:
I place my palms along your shoulder blades
and become a pair of wings.
We move out of this life
like an ocean in peacetime,
our bones, the ribs, fanning inland
until dying things seem
as small as the light between them.

The Snow Will Speak

My lover tells me his mother
had only one arm
to hold him.
           That is his reason
for drawing me so tightly
into his wide chest.
           And there, squeezed between
his flannel shoulder and pocket,
I am too considerate to ask

           the obvious questions,
such as, how did she cook dinner, or,
how did you board the trolley together
with your groceries and schoolbooks?

Outside, ice is sealing
the tips of trees, the sky and snow
have become the same shade of blue.
           To not be hurt,
she wore red lipstick
and whistled, he claims.
           Sometimes the wind caught
one of her seersucker dresses and filled it
like a bell.

On the next block, a shovel cuts
into asphalt, scraping
its tune of long weather.
           Soon the snow will drift
up my rickety stairs
like a voice which speaks when I can't.

Picnic

On a small beach where everyone returned
after failure in a decade of winters,
our immigrant friend
refused to pull himself out of the rain
because it was our first summer picnic
with smoked kielbasa and hot drippy sauerkraut.
Along the shoreline, near the stinky grasses,
he stood on his head in the water
like a fool, breaking the sky with his legs.
I said nothing even though I saw
the wet air pass over us in one dumb blessing.
Somehow I knew there were things without words.
Under a bedsheet tied like a tent
I opened my palms
as wide as the Michigan plains,
and watched the child my mother
shielded from the rain
curl himself into a ball,
one of those round shy bugs in June,
never speaking the rest of his life.

Grace

Air begins a season of night.
Crevices all over the earth are turning inward.
The wind is throwing wheat and dust in a fit of absolution,
and I may be a Puritan child
waking again in a bed of jimson weed.
Can it still be this way, I ask,
places all over the earth that cannot be touched?
Now I rise and walk in a month of black air,
releasing small animals in my step.
What is this darkness gathering with my legs,
is it sin?
I know the signs of discord, I know them like
my left palm,
these dull stones and trees expressing waves of steam.
Now they are whispering
of a plan for me:
something called grace.
Yet beyond the forest I see men raking
a field of smoking furs,
forgetting the country stolen from them.
This is not my land.
This belongs to other creatures
waking in their own skin.
Here is the beginning of my betrayal
which will last a lifetime.
No water I find will wash it
and no stone I touch will return me.
I want to hold my clothes against myself
like a thief in a crowd of strangers,
another body among the trees.

Blinding the Horse

Cover his eyes with a white rag
His mane will not blaze
Lead him into
the brittle night & air
full of singed hay
The barn is burning
yet for a moment it stands

Fire is so much like love

First the beams flaring
then falling
then the roof slowly breaking
in half over the oiled floor
Such light for the soul
blind and waiting
in the cool trees

The Water Basket Vision

In the Yucatan, there are no rivers above ground

What cannot be seen
is a room of dust between my hipbones
where a woman lies giving birth
to one damaged child after the other.

If she can't think of names,
her Mayan clansmen will invent a codex
of tangled legs and faces in the sand.

Withered trout fins are a picture
of her last son, wrapped in a straw
burial basket and laid beside the longest
river in the world,
head pointed downstream,
the direction of water flowing from its source.

My worst dream is that the river begins anywhere.
I know birth is a mouth at this river,
a spine unfolding into daylight and passage,
the familiar head and hands,
the fertile crease.
But I am afraid of accidents,
the single eclipse in time
when a woman must retrace water backwards,
counting the days it takes

for skin to weave itself
until her basket vanishes,
without the human child
and she is almost incomprehensible,
turning all colors of the earth in grief.

Elegy

The day he parted
his body from hers
she folded pieces of tissue paper
between the sleeves and lapel
of his best dark suit
and packed it with the rest
of her clothes
to carry
across the country
on this cold train
this slender grey dream we travel
Each of us has formed a small room all our own
between the seat ahead
and the land rising and dipping
out the window
Soon we will become like one another
stretching for oxygen
lifting coffee to our lips
watching small cattle
kick their heels in the wake
of our train
until our heads fall
slanted in one direction
against the clouded glass
like rain riding over the flatlands
Tonight we follow a steel arch
above a red industrial arm
hammering past midnight
and above tight highway houses
I think I know why she grieves
even though it was not the first death

Somewhere else the rain may be holding light
in a cradle of wet earth
but now there is nothing
between her body
and the world

Fragments

I

In a picture from 1939,
the face of my father resembles
his favorite aunt
standing behind him on her back porch.
Their bones are even, shoulder to shin.
Her head touches his. It may be
late morning. My father
has hitched from Michigan to Missouri
to see her, a year after the dustbowl.
Scorched, vengeful land rests in the distance.
At thirteen he didn't know
what made him light out.
Six-hundred miles south he wired her,
and she met him there, half way up a dirt highway,
when he was voiceless, feverish,
and without a dime in his last innocence.

II

We know the coming of war
in the hesitant lungs of a child's cough.
While my father slept inside a brown muffler
his aunt had wrapped him in,
the wool becoming thicker and thicker
around his throat,
Hitler was mapping the countryside
of Europe in iron chains.
It took years.
Metal on metal sliding against the snow
is a sound which never ends.

I think it stays in the earth forever
until other sounds join it:
terror and memory, a pair of deer
slipping too cautiously through the cold air.

III

Two lean figures with straight hair
are watching color lift off the earth.
In five years the beams
of this house would sway too far an angle
to be restored. My father would be
waving down a bus for Texas and the army.
Snow would fall into the eyes of Europeans.
But in the winter of this picture
he is almost the figure I've always known,
someone who wants to go home when
everything is finished, someone
who couldn't answer the long,
starved sky, or the wind,
mourning like a parent.

My Grandmother Dreams of Dying Young

As I zip her dress
she tells me to look for the bruise
between her shoulders
and think of her as a girl
walking in a yard of young animals.
It is early evening and the cows still carry
a haze of grain on their lips.
My grandmother is wearing wool stockings and black boots.
Pieces of bone and teeth from the autumn slaughter
are scattered in the grass,
but as she walks the fog is filling
her hair with water.
She hears a man motioning behind her,
now bending to tie his shoe
now clearing his throat   now watching her chin incline
now extending his palm as if to plane the back of her neck.
But as she takes him
he slowly turns white beside her
leaving the shape of his skull on her pillowcase.
For years she guides her hand
underneath the cloth as if
she could reach the outline of his face.
And the hand now wrinkled, chilled,
withdraws as untouched as the pale boards
surrounding a hollow window.
This was before the war. The buckets were heavy.
The worn length from the house to the barn
gave itself up completely to the rain.
When she fell the elder aunts rushed to her,
crossed themselves, and wrapped her in sheets.
The dark space on her back she says is where they held her
as they picked her up and put her down because
she was empty, weightless, and remembered nothing at all.

'the homesick traveler thinks of oranges'

Thinking of rain
how it poured over our east field
making one long eddy down the center;
those pigeons who gobbled your discarded bread
are dipping in and out of puddles.
This spring rain they have become
kingfishers plunging for worms.
Everything smells of worms,
and rawness.

I used to let my mother go on about
the kudzu vines and oranges in Florida.
When they gathered Spanish moss from the trees
she said, it was like shaving old men.
My mother hid a baby iguana underneath her house,
and caught flies at night to feed it.
I listen because I am so tired of losing.

And there is a cavern I follow
from the bridge of her nose
deep into her eye,
where I believe the sight
of a small kimonoed woman
bowing into the river and the sun,
calling a carp with the clap of her hands.

Before My Birth, You Dream of Me

for my mother

You want to run your hand along the tracks
and touch all the old hoboes
who came there to sleep or die;
you would tuck their knees underneath their chins
and help them curl away from the rain.
They would be no more unusual than those small
brown buckeyes discovered between the slats.
But coming to your own body,
I think you are hit
by something so strange it almost scares you,
your husband's dark shape is suddenly too distant,
and you see yourself one night shifting next to him,
quietly adding another to yourself.
Wakening, you are all folded in the same direction,
your husband, your child, and the hoboes.

In another dream, your hand follows a young girl
through a row of clapboard warehouses
to an empty platform where she waits all night
for snow to arrive on top an engine from the north.
But the snow has melted,
and she will never see snow in her life.
The old men spit on the rails and tell you
it is only your hand following her back,
your hand grazing the ground,
searching for something young,
a child who may have fallen against the tracks.

All through the dream you imagine
this young girl's life has passed out of your hands
or that you never even held it,
until across the railyard a whistle sounds,
your head shifts, the grasses part.
You see her eyes opening,
she sees a bevy of quail rising beyond the tracks.

Seascape

for Jeanne

That summer we came to the shore many times.
Once we watched while a palsied child
was lifted to a flannel blanket
spread over the sand.
She had left her wheelchair
with the beach toys,
bright gleaming pieces in the high sun.
While other children shrieked, stampeding
over candy papers and wax cups,
a mother could not read her magazine
and a father fumbled alone with a picnic basket.
As a salt wave rose to wind,
every inch of the white tide exhaling caution,
nearer us the water curled
its moon snails and marl, then unfolded
out to sea again.
Using her bent, misshapen arms,
she slowly scooted her whole cambered body
closer to the calm tide
where others waited to take her in.
We watched her as we watched the sea,
and I turned to ask you if these clouds
pausing and then separating overhead
were really a mirage
forming the eye of our heart,
the widening sky and the soft water
were all around us,
and there were her pale arms flailing
in their own language
as she gazed at the wild tern,
fascinated by a bird's slow wing
cutting the blue air.

My Brother's Shirt

Lately I've been wearing my brother's shirt,
a threadbare cotton, windowpane check,
a shirt the milkman coaching Little League
in the heat would wear.
I leave the first two buttons undone,
imagining that my long, tan arms
winging out of these cool sleeves
must be like my brother's when he was a little boy.
Now the shirt is old and soft,
and there is no one else around except me.
Out of my window the sky has acquired
for a few minutes, that clear, vertical blue,
a color identical to childhood.
I wish my words could be as direct
as that hue,
and as unambiguous.
If the earth with all of its water
and continents were really
the figure of a human being,
and the atmosphere hanging above it
were the articulate visions
dreamed by that human—
but this is not the truth.
Actually, my words will always be
as lost and chaotic as the world.
Around the collar my brother's name
is written in fifteen year old ink
that has never washed out.
He wore this shirt during those years
he lived in an institution for the retarded,
a place where there is no childhood, really,

only a congregation with other
contorted arms and legs,
and their moaning, slow moving heads above
bodies without age.
In the same drawstring pants
and square shirt I am wearing now,
the boy with red patchy skin
looked just like my brother, whose graceful
head and olive color were undistinguished
in these clothes.
To prevent lice, they cut the younger
boys' hair very close to the skull.
The whole time he was there my brother
never wore a pair of shoes which fit him.
But he was two hundred miles
from me, in the flat Michigan country
of sugar beets and scrap metal.
The institution was once an army base
and he slept in one of those rod beds,
on his back, like a soldier, I think,
meditatively grazing his fingers
over the floor dust.
On our trips to visit, I always thought
the endless rows of barracks were not green
at all, but the yellow of scrambled eggs
and pocked by peeled chips of paint
which were floating to nearby rose gardens
and down the river to the city of Kalamazoo.
When we finally turned into the long road
leading there, I would see him, yards and yards
ahead of us, swaying back and forth, drinking
Coca-cola beside a mute, wide-eyed girl.
Not far from here, and unseen from the highway
were woods, my mother told me.
My brother loved the woods, the multiple trees
and sudden fields of weeds.

Once outside, he would eat the tops of flowers
or stuff himself with grasses until
his mouth was stained
that light, telltale green.
At this place, she had suggested,
he would be able to walk out
into the trees from his back door.
Now I am old enough to know why
she was lying to me,
and why she continued this small, soothing
tale year after year,
but what I don't know is why
that word sorrow, so thick and weighted,
the sound of melancholy,
the one I can repeat over
and over so clearly now,
had not entered me that day.
I must have been a child who did not have
enough words yet, joining a brother who
would never speak with words.
We only knew what we could see and touch,
a soft cotton shirt, our brown arms.
The sky was that vivid, remarkable blue.
And on the other side of the veterans' graveyard,
over a hill of symmetrical white crosses,
a body of water for these silent children to swim
lay flattened out against the sky.

POETRY FROM ALICE JAMES BOOKS